Activity Book

★	Hello!	2
1	Getting around	6
2	People and places	12
★	Review Units 1 and 2	18
3	Making plans	20
4	Healthy body, healthy mind	26
★	Review Units 3 and 4	32
5	Our changing world	34

6	Flying high	40
★	Review Units 5 and 6	46
7	Stars in their eyes	48
8	Journeys	54
★	Review Units 7 and 8	60
	Christmas	62
	Valentine's Day	63
	Earth Day	64

Hello!

1 **Read and complete.**

sister	eleven	~~Ben~~
	Brentwood School	

Hi! I'm _Ben_.
I'm _____ .
I go to _____ _____ .
I've got a _____ .

Draw a picture and write about yourself.

Hi! _____
_____
_____
_____ .

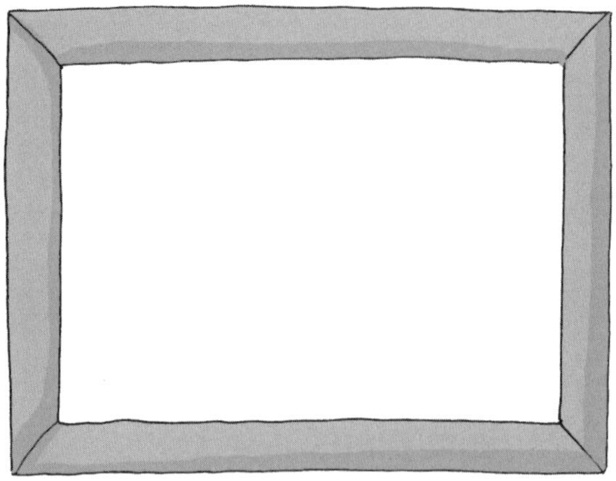

2 **Colour and write.**

14 13 11 12 15
fourteen thirteen eleven twelve fifteen

Complete the sentences.

1 The twins are _____ .

2 Oscar is _____ .

3 I'm _____ .

3 **Find the missing word.**

Ben, Gina, Oscar and Tessa are _____ . srefnid

2

4 ✏️ What's in Ben's bag?

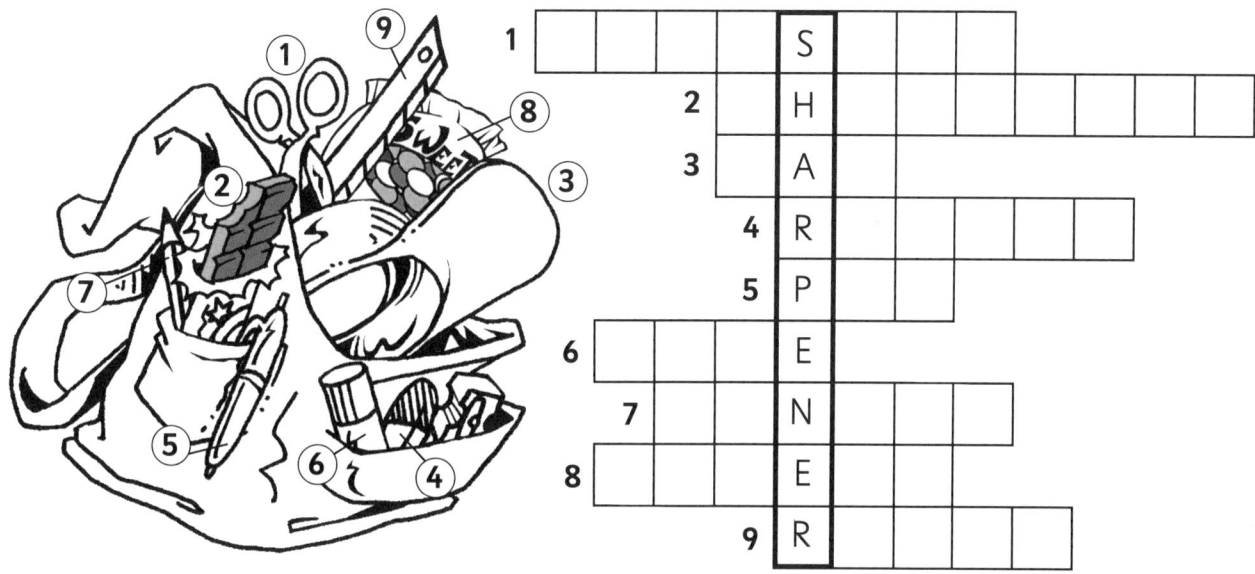

5 📼 Listen and draw.

6 ✏️ Look and answer the questions.

1 Where's the cat? ___It's_____ .
2 Where are the sweets? ___They're_____ .
3 Where's the pencil case? _____ .
4 Where are the books? _____ .

7. Classify and write two more words.

Saturday   Maths   ~~September~~
Tuesday   February   Geography
Thursday   July   Art

Months   **Days**   **Subjects**

September

8. What are they saying? Look and write.

drawing   swimming   reading   singing   ~~playing football~~

1. I like _playing football_.

2.

3.

4.

5.

9 🎧 **Listen and tick.**

	🐕	🐈	🐁
Tessa			
Ben			
Gina			

10 ✏️ **Circle the true sentences.**

1 Tessa's got a dog.

2 Gina's got a mouse.

3 Ben's got a cat.

4 Ben and Gina have got a dog.

5 Tessa hasn't got a cat.

11 ✏️ **Where do they sleep? Look and write.**

1    3

2   4

1 *The rabbit sleeps in a basket.*
2 _____ .
3 _____ .
4 _____ .

1 Getting around

1 How do they go to school? Find and write.

1 _She goes to school by_ _____.
2 _____.
3 _____.
4 _____.

2 Write the question in the correct order.

do you to go How ? school

_____
_____

Now answer the question.

_I go_ _____.

3 Now ask your friends and complete the survey. Use colours.

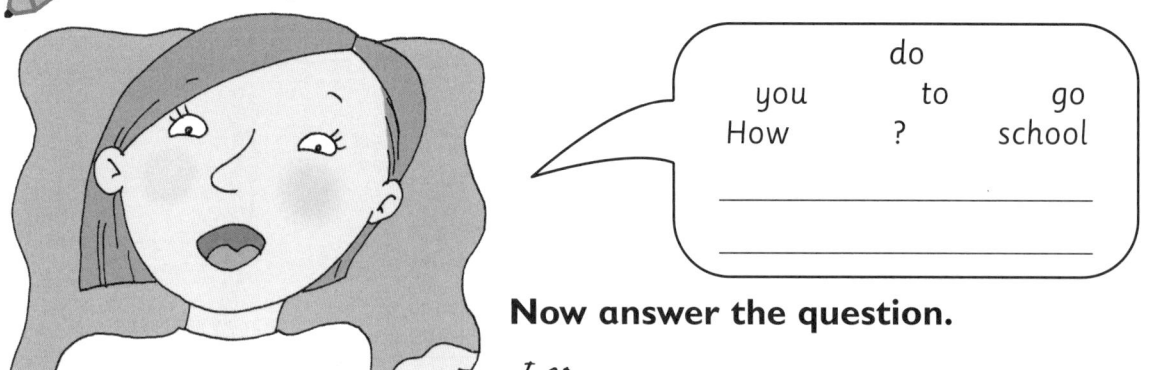

6

Where do they live? Look and write.

1. _She lives near the airport_.
2. _____.

3. _____.
4. _____.

Answer the question.

Where do you live?   I live near the _____.

 **Look and write.**

| Yes, he does | ~~No, he doesn't~~ |
| Yes, she does | No, she doesn't |

 He goes by bus.
No, he doesn't.

 She goes to school by bike.
_____.

 She goes by train.
_____.

 He goes by Underground.
_____.

 Circle the odd ones out.

train / park / station

airport / school / plane

bus / shop / bus stop

7

7 Who is speaking? Kronk or the men?

1 Don't turn right at the tree!

2 Then go up the little path to the top.

3 Excuse me. We're looking for Pacha's house.

4 Go across the stream.

8 Read and circle the correct words.

1 The two friends are looking for (Pacha's house) / the station.
2 They turn **right** / **left** at the **corner shop** / **big tree**.
3 They go up the **path** / **hill** and turn **right** / **left**.
4 Oh, no, there's a problem – **quicksand** / **a river**!

9 Write a story. Use the words not circled in Activity 8.

1 The two friends are looking for the station.

2 _____

3 _____

4 _____

Now tick the solution.

The friends can swim. ☐   They see a bridge. ☐

They cross the river on stepping stones. ☐

10  Right or left? Look and write.

1 PARK — *Turn right for the park.*

2 STATION — _____.

3 RIVER — _____.

4 HILL — _____.

11 Find the box. Listen and mark the route.

The box is in the _____.

12   What's in the box? Look at the code and write.

It's a

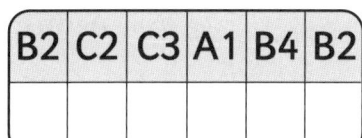

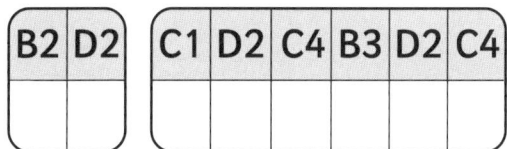

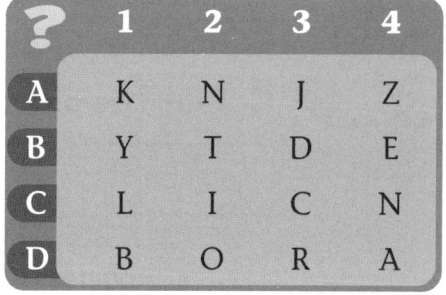

Find and write the words.

C	A	T	F	I	R	F		I	H	S	T	G	L

Now find the words and colour the lights.

1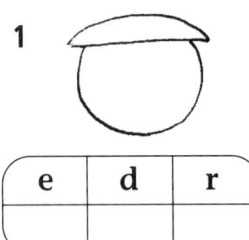

e	d	r

2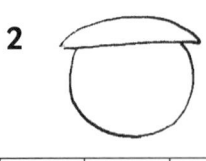

r	b	a	e	m

3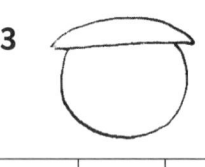

r	e	g	e	n

Fill in the sentences.

4 Stop at the _____ light.   5 Go at the _____ light.

  Look and write.

Go to the big _____ (1) . Turn _____ (2) . Walk to the _____ (3) _____ (4) . Turn _____ (5) . The bike's on the _____ (6) , near the _____ (7) .

Colour the places in red, the transport in blue.

station   bus   park   school

plane   train   shop   boat

16 Complete and write the words.

```
        T
      _ r _ _ _ _ _ _
    _ _ a _ _
      _ n _ _ _ _ _ _ _ _ _
    _ _ s
        p _ _ _ _
      _ o _ _
      _ _ r
        t _ _ _
```

- boat
- traffic
- plane
- bus
- taxi
- train
- Underground
- car

17 Complete and answer.

1 *Excuse me* . *Where* _____ ?   _____ _____ .
2 _____ ?   _____ _____ .
3 _____ ?   _____ _____ .

English Adventure

Self evaluation. Read, think and shade the YES.

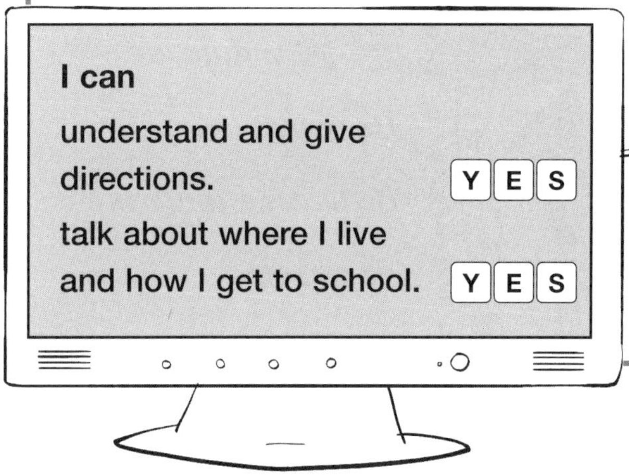

I can
understand and give directions. [Y][E][S]
talk about where I live and how I get to school. [Y][E][S]

Make a word and complete the sentence.
I'm _ _ _ _ _ .

2 People and places

1 What do they want to be?

1 She wants to be _____.

2 He _____.

3 _____.

4 _____.

What do you want to be? _____.

2 Circle the people who work in a school.

| nurse | cleaner | singer | reporter |
| teacher | pilot | cook | secretary |

3 What does a pilot do? Write true sentences.

He works at weekends.

His job is difficult.

He makes cakes.

He wears a uniform.

He travels.

He dances and sings.

_____.

_____.

_____.

_____.

4 Match.

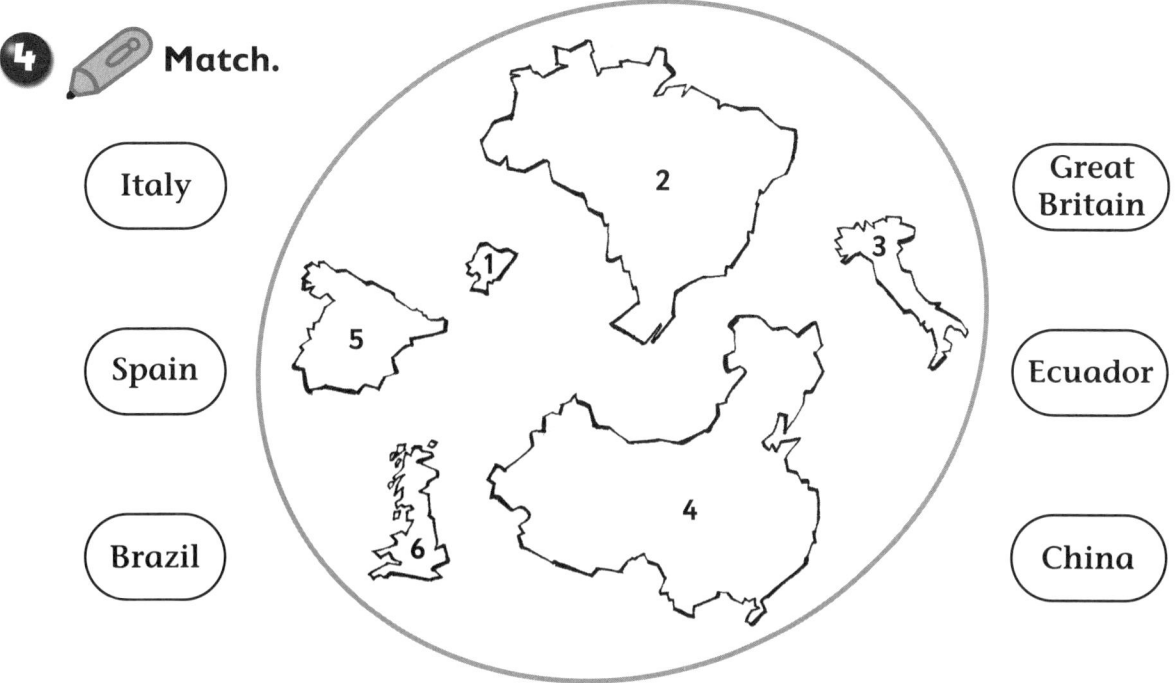

- Italy
- Spain
- Brazil
- Great Britain
- Ecuador
- China

What other countries do you know?

5 Where are they from?

1. tniBair teraG — She's from Great Britain.

2. lBrzai — _____.

3. Cianh — _____.

4. curaodE — _____.

5. Sapin — _____.

6. ltyIa — _____.

6 Who's speaking? Write *Audrey* or *Milo*.

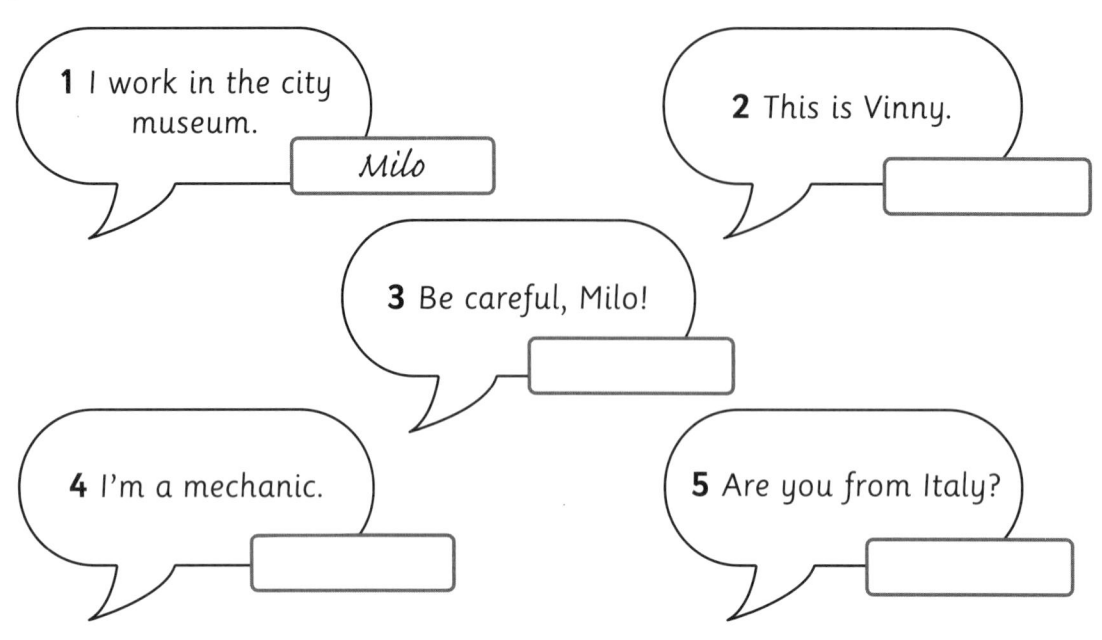

1 I work in the city museum. Milo

2 This is Vinny. ____

3 Be careful, Milo! ____

4 I'm a mechanic. ____

5 Are you from Italy? ____

7 Choose and write the correct answers.

| Yes, of course | ~~My name's Milo~~ |
| A geologist studies rocks and soil | France | I'm a geologist |

1 What's your name? _My name's Milo._
2 Where are you from? _____.
3 What do you do? _____.
4 What's a geologist? _____.
5 Can I look at your rocks? _____.

Now act out the conversation with a friend.

8 Tick the words that you can make from *geologist*.

soil ☐   go ☐   rock ☐   sit ☐
hole ☐   egg ☐   toe ☐   look ☐

Find and write another word. _____

9 Complete.

| I'm | He's | She's | We're |

1. 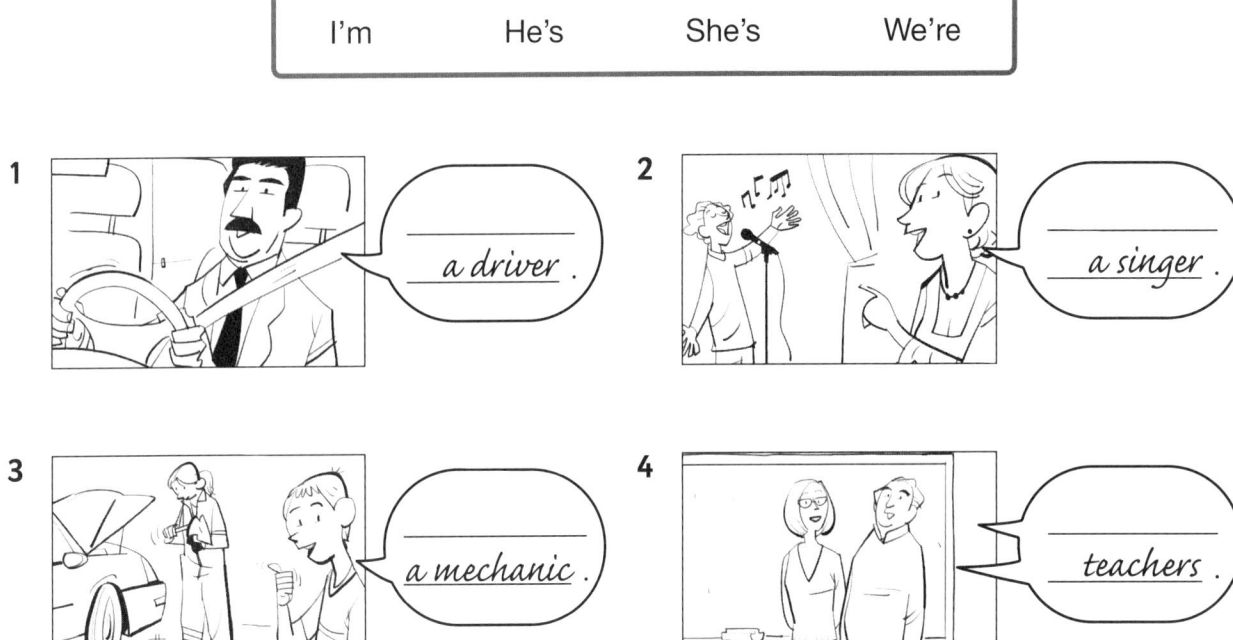 _He's_ a driver.
2. _She's_ a singer.
3. _He's_ a mechanic.
4. _We're_ teachers.

10 Who's speaking? Listen and number.

11 Circle the correct words.

1 I'm a cook; I **work** / **don't work** in a kitchen.

2 I'm a pilot; I **travel** / **don't travel**.

3 I'm a teacher; I **work** / **don't work** in a hospital.

4 I'm a reporter; I **speak** / **don't speak** English.

15

12 Match the countries and nationalities.

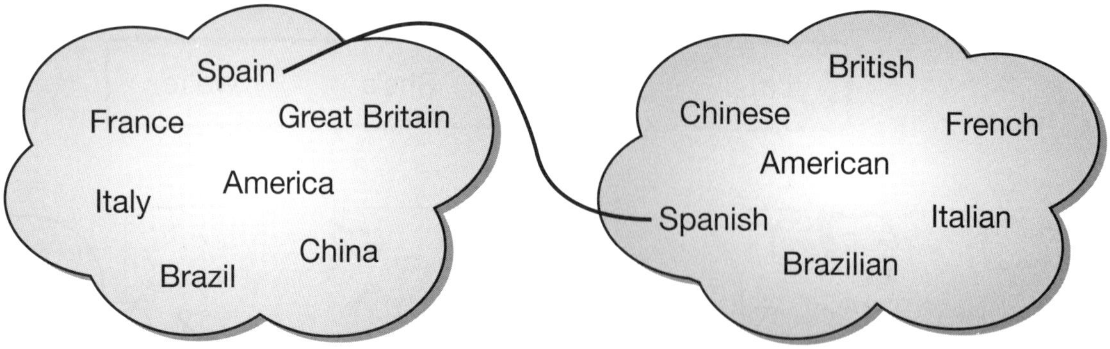

Spain France Great Britain Italy America China Brazil

British Chinese French American Spanish Italian Brazilian

13 Throw a coin to find out about your Mystery Man.

1 Does he live alone? _____ .
2 Does he drive a car? _____ .
3 Does he speak Italian? _____ .
4 Does he work all day? _____ .
5 Does he play the guitar? _____ .

Heads = Yes, he does.

Tails = No, he doesn't.

14 Draw and write about your Mystery Man.

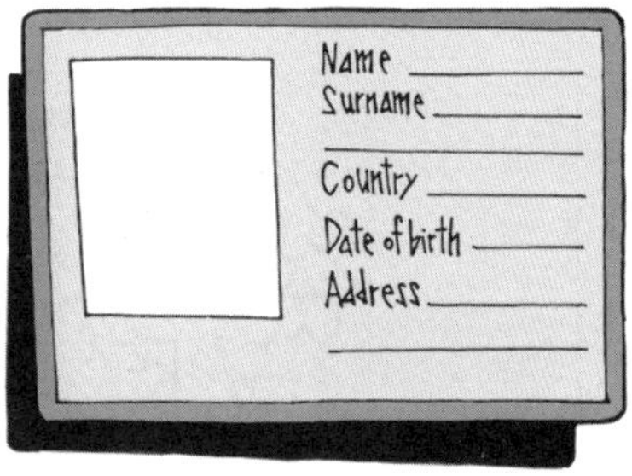

Name
Surname
Country
Date of birth
Address

His name's _____
_____
_____
_____
_____ .

15 Find eight jobs. Write the words.

S	I	N	G	E	R	I	M
E	N	P	I	F	L	D	T
C	S	I	M	D	I	O	E
R	O	L	B	A	E	C	A
E	S	O	W	N	S	T	C
T	K	T	K	C	S	O	H
A	T	O	N	E	V	R	E
R	E	P	O	R	T	E	R
Y	D	E	N	T	I	S	T

Secretary
_____
_____
_____
_____
_____
_____
_____

16

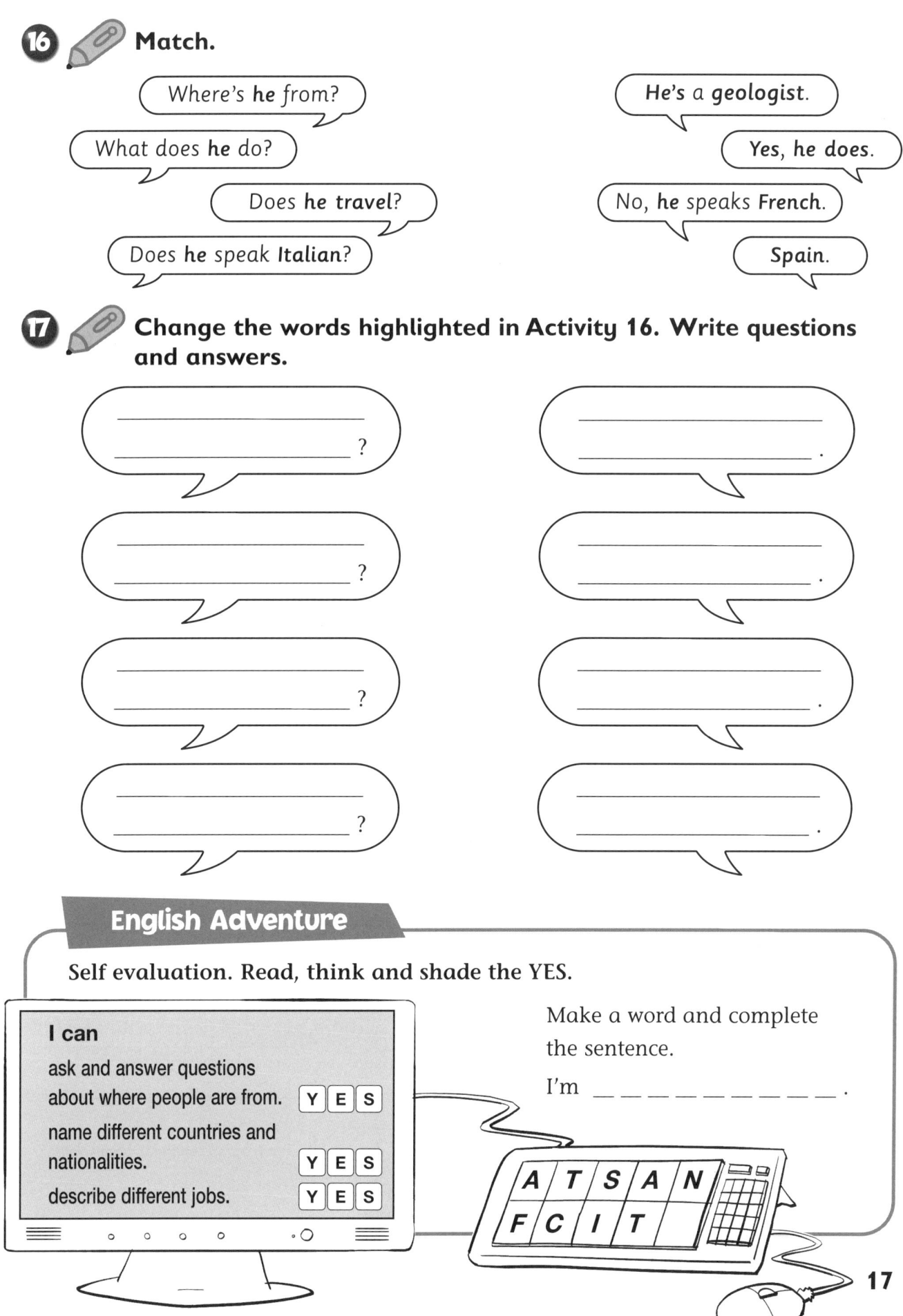

Review
Units 1 and 2

1 🎧 **Listen and complete the signpost.**

Underground
station
park
hospital

2 ✏️ **Find seven countries.**

F	R	A	N	C	E	B
S	I	K	L	M	S	R
P	M	C	H	I	N	A
A	P	W	T	G	E	Z
I	T	A	L	Y	M	I
N	S	N	G	H	P	L
E	C	U	A	D	O	R
B	R	I	T	A	I	N

3 ✏️ **Find and write.**

1 The nurse is Chinese.
2 _____.
3 _____.
4 _____.

18

4. Read and complete.

| night | office | English | children | work | travel |

1. I don't work in an _____ .
   I work with _____ .

2. I _____ in a hospital.
   I work at _____ .

3. I _____ to many countries.
   I speak _____ .

5. Write.

1. _____
2. _____
3. _____
4. _____
5. _____
6. _____
7. _____
8. _____

3 Making plans

1 ✏️ **What are they going to do? Look and write.**

She's going to play tennis.

_____.

_____.

_____.

2 📖 **What's Luke going to do? Look and read.**

I'm going to win the next Olympics!

ACTION PLAN
Jog in the park
Swim in the pool
Walk to school
Do press-ups
Climb ropes
Lift weights

Write about what Luke is going to do.

1 He's _____.
2 _____.
3 _____.
4 _____.
5 _____.
6 _____.

20

3 Find and write the words.

ssgsslaune
sunglasses

oollnsab
_____

pperwsneas
_____

vitniinsoat
_____

dofo
_____

kdrni
_____

scimu
_____

4 Look and write.

Some children are going to have a party. What do they need? Look at the pictures in Activity 3 and write ✗ or ✓. Then complete the sentences.

1 _They are going to need_ _____.
2 _But they are not going to need_ _____.

5 What are you going to do? Choose.

1 I'm going to be a photographer.

2 I'm going to learn to paint.

3 I'm going to have a party.

Choose your action plan and write.

| buy a camera | invite my friends | go to Art classes |
| make a cake | take photos | visit the art gallery |

I'm going to _____.
_____.

21

6 Write the sentences correctly. Tick the true ones.

party townspeople going to are have The a

1 *The townspeople are going to have a party.*

save The is hydra going the to town

2 _____.

to is going dance all Hercules night

3 _____.

the Hercules going fight hydra to is

4 _____.

The hide going is to hydra

5 _____.

7 Read and circle the correct words.

The townspeople are going to **fight** / **celebrate**. They're going to invite Hercules to their **party** / **battle**. They're going to **hide** / **eat** sandwiches and they're going to **dance** / **play golf**. They're going to have **fun** / **a bath**.

8 Read and answer in complete sentences.

1 Who is going to celebrate? _____.
2 What are they going to eat? _____.
3 What are they going to do? _____.
4 Who is going to come to the party? _____.

22

13 🎧 **What are they going to take on the trip? Listen and fill in the chart.**

	Yes	No
sweets		
camera		
torch		
sleeping bag		
sunglasses		

14 ✏️ **What's Tessa going to do on Saturday?**

On Saturday, Tessa _____
_____
_____
_____
_____ .

SATURDAY
visit Granny
buy a present for Mum
watch the match
do homework

SUN

15 ✏️ **What are you going to do on Saturday?**

On Saturday, I'm _____
_____ .

Now ask a friend and write.

My friend's _____
_____ .

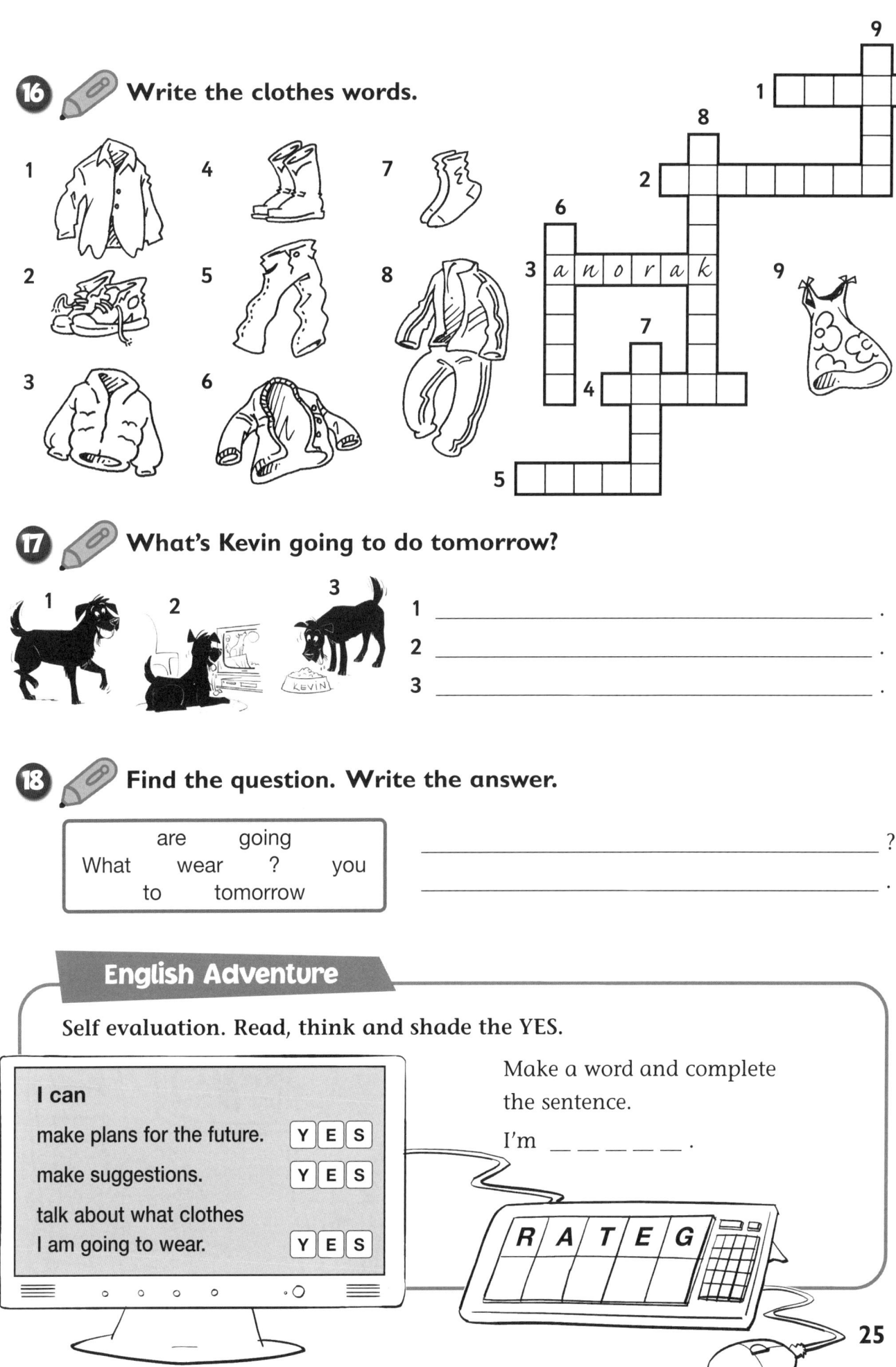

4 Healthy body, healthy mind

1 🎧 **Listen and number.**

2 ✏️ **Label.**

oil   vinegar   salt   pepper

oil

3 ✏️ **Read and match.**

1 Don't open it!

2 Don't sit on the chair!

3 Don't drink that!

26

4 ✏️ **Complete the food words.**

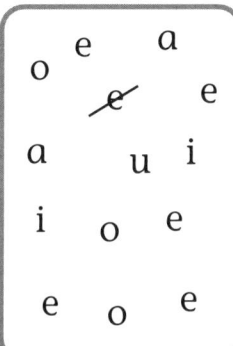

Circle the food you eat every day in red.

_e_ g g s

t _ _ s t

f r _ _ t

c h _ _ s _

c h _ c k _ n

c h _ c _ l _ t _

5 ✏️ **What do you have for breakfast?**

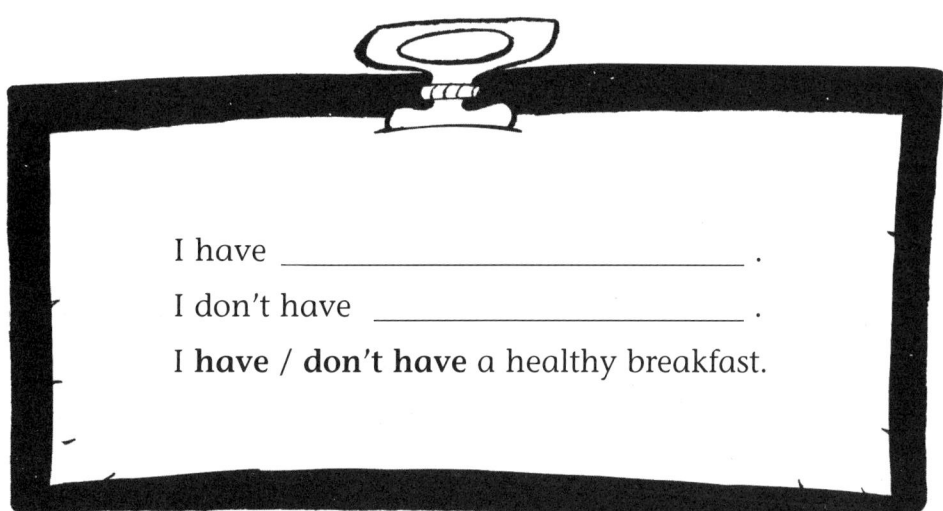

I have _____ .
I don't have _____ .
I **have** / **don't have** a healthy breakfast.

6 ✏️ **What do your friends have for breakfast? Write the names.**

Find someone who has:

eggs	toast	cheese
_____	_____	_____
milk	cakes	orange juice
_____	_____	_____
cereal	biscuits	yoghurt
_____	_____	_____

27

7 **Which does Kuzco say? Read and tick.**

1 Give me soup. ☐
2 Give me a bug. ☐
3 Give me a salad. ☐
4 Give me a pie. ☐
5 Give me a spider. ☐
6 Give me a fly. ☐

8 **Can you remember? Answer in complete sentences.**

1 Who's hungry? _____ .
2 Where do they go? _____ .
3 Who brings the food? _____ .
4 What does she bring? _____ .
5 What does Pacha do? _____ .

9 **Read, match and complete the pictures.**

1 Oh, no! There's a fly in my soup!

2 Oh, no! There's a bug on the table!

3 Oh, no! There's a spider in the fruit basket!

10 🎧 **Listen and colour the game.**

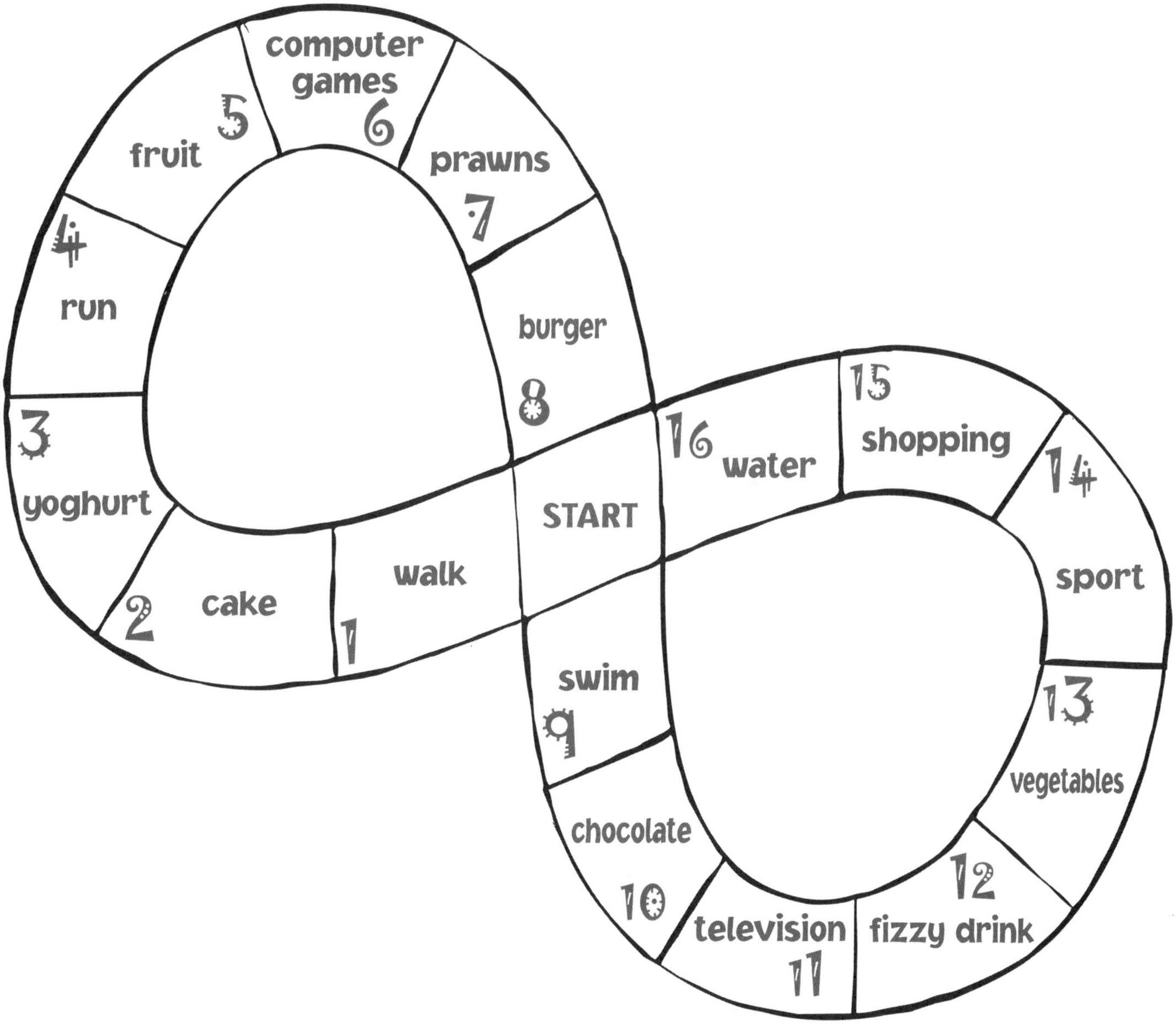

(Game board: 1 walk, 2 cake, 3 yoghurt, 4 run, 5 fruit, 6 computer games, 7 prawns, 8 burger, START, 9 swim, 10 chocolate, 11 television, 12 fizzy drink, 13 vegetables, 14 sport, 15 shopping, 16 water)

11 🎲 **Play the game with a friend.**

How to play.
1 Put a counter on start.
2 Throw the dice.
3 Tick the score card of the same colour as your square.
4 Go round three times.
5 Now count the ticks in your score card.

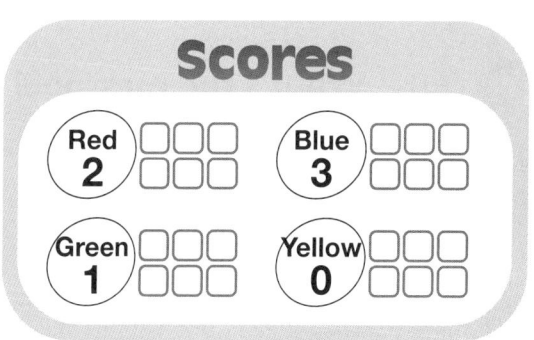

Scores
Red 2
Blue 3
Green 1
Yellow 0

12 **Where do you do these things? Classify.**

	bedroom	bathroom	kitchen
have a shower		✓	
go to sleep			
eat your toast			
have a salad			
get dressed			
clean your teeth			

Add one more activity for each room.

13 **Match.**

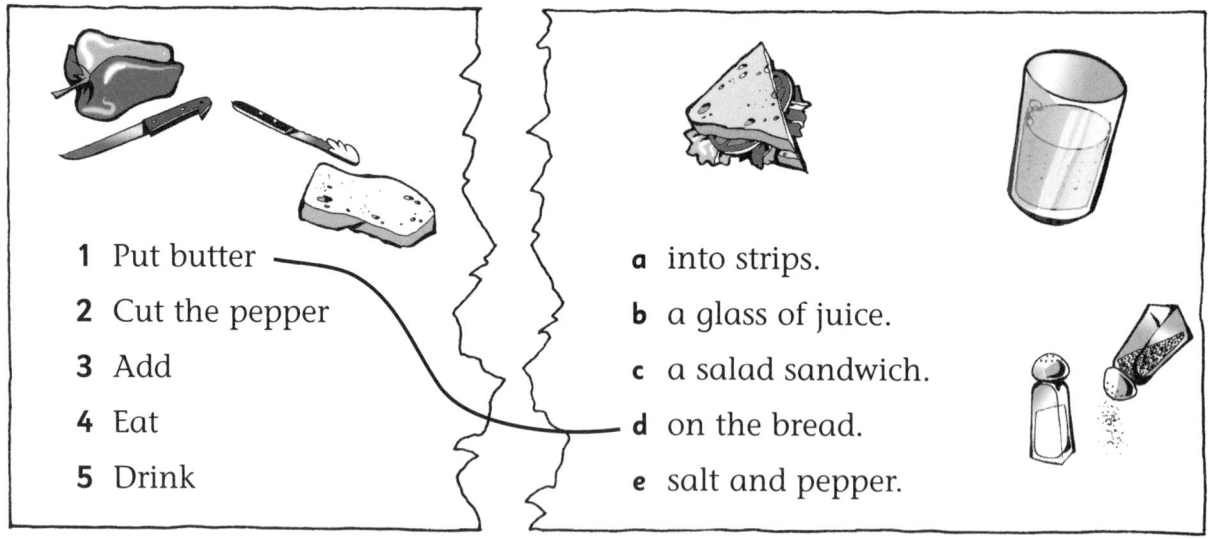

1 Put butter
2 Cut the pepper
3 Add
4 Eat
5 Drink

a into strips.
b a glass of juice.
c a salad sandwich.
d on the bread.
e salt and pepper.

14  **What's the message? Listen and write the code.**

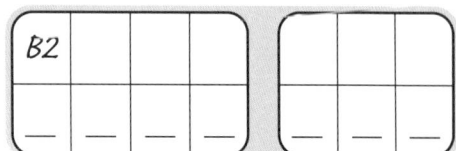

?	1	2	3	4
A	F	B	E	N
B	M	K	T	A
C	I	R	L	P

B2 _ _ _ _   _ _ _

15 Read and match.

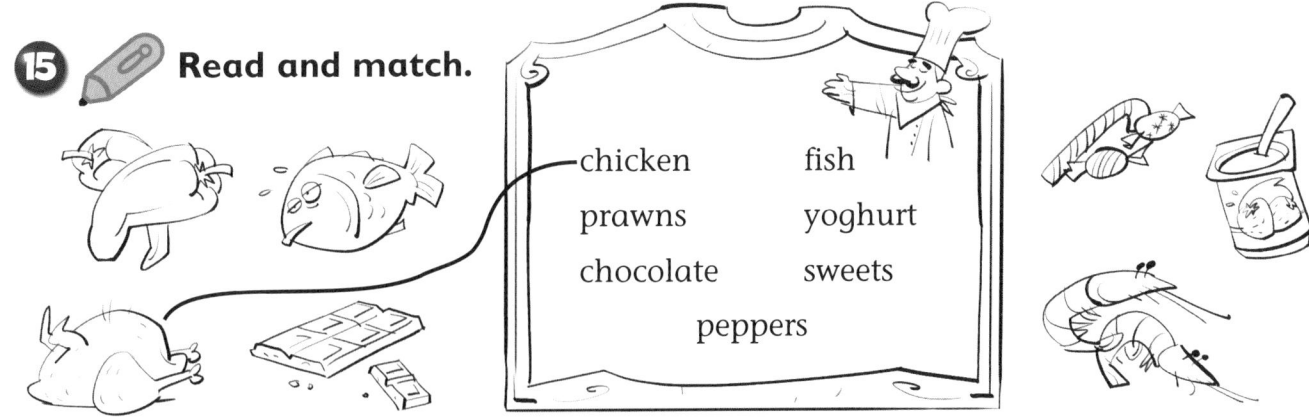

chicken fish
prawns yoghurt
chocolate sweets
peppers

Which foods can we add to rice? Circle.

16 Keep fit! Fill in the chart.

✗	✓
Don't go by bus.	Walk to school.

17 Order and complete the recipe.

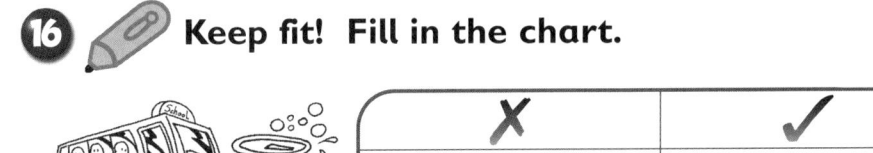

First   Then   Next   Finally

_____ wash the lettuce. ☐   _____ eat the salad. ☐
_____ add oil and vinegar. ☐   _____ cut the tomatoes. ☐

English Adventure

Self evaluation. Read, think and shade the YES.

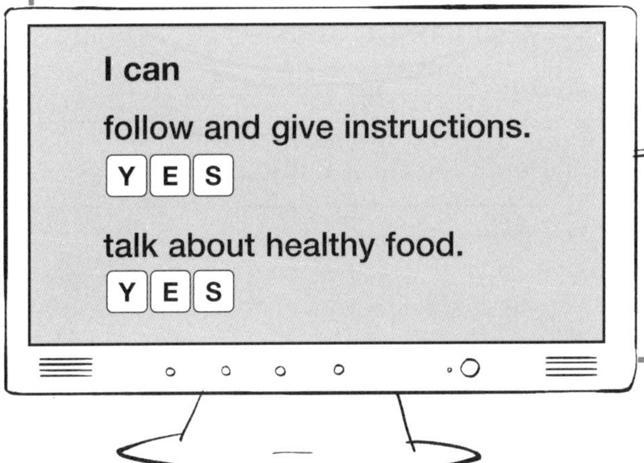

I can

follow and give instructions.
Y E S

talk about healthy food.
Y E S

Make a word and complete the sentence.
I'm a _ _ _ _ _ _ _ _ .

H A P M I
O C N

Review
Units 3 and 4

1 **What's Tessa going to do on Saturday? Look and write.**

Saturday
- clean her room ✓
- write e-mails ✗
- buy a CD ✗
- wash her sports clothes ✓
- phone her granny ✓
- visit her friends ✗

1 *She's going to clean her room, but she isn't going to write e-mails.*

2 _____

3 _____

2 **Write true (T) or false (F)?**

1 Dogs don't speak English. ☐ *T*
2 Trees are purple. ☐
3 Planes don't fly. ☐
4 Families live in houses. ☐
5 Buses don't have windows. ☐

3 **Read and draw.**

1 Eat the fish, please!

2 Eat your eggs, please!

3 Drink your milk, please!

4 Here's the cake! Cut it, please!

4. Read and write the missing words.

Barbie is a _photographer_. She's from London. She lives near the _____ with her _____.

Next week she's going to _____. She's not going to eat _____ and _____ _____.

She's going to _____ _____. She's going to pack her _____ and _____. She's going to get the _____ to the airport. She isn't going to take the _____.

5. Read the questions. Choose and answer five.

1 Where's Barbie from?
2 Where does she live?
3 Has she got a pet?
4 Is she going to go to France?
5 Is she going to eat pizza?
6 What's she going to do?
7 What's she going to take?
8 Where's the train going to take her?
9 Is she going to take the dogs?

1. She's from London.

5 Our changing world

1 ✎ **Complete.**

1 There was a swing.
2 There _____ a slide.
3 There was _____ pond.
4 There _____ ducks in the pond.
5 There were children on the _____ .
6 There _____ a boy on the _____ .

2 ✎ **What is there now?**

There's a | p | p | i | h | o | s | g | n | | r | t | c | n | e | e |

3 🔊 **Listen. Tick the animals that were there.**

34

4 Match.

very windy

very dry

very wet

flood

hurricane

drought

5 Complete.

1 1995 = nineteen ninety- _____
2 1860 = _____ sixty
3 2002 = two _____ and _____
4 1988 = _____ _____ - eight

What year is it now? _____

6 Answer the questions.

Yes, it was   No, it wasn't

Monday
Tuesday
Wednesday
Thursday
Friday
Saturday
Sunday

1 Was it sunny on Monday?
   _____ .

2 Was it windy on Tuesday?
   _____ .

3 Was it cloudy on Saturday?
   _____ .

35

7 Read and circle the correct words.

Life was (good) / difficult in the valley / mountain. There was a beautiful lake / park. The lemurs / dolphins played in the lake / swimming pool. Yar's island / forest was beautiful too. One day there were lights / floods in the sky / field. A fireball / hurricane crashed into the sea / trees and destroyed the island.

8 Write *true* (T) or *false* (F)?

1 Baylene jumped into the lake. [T]
2 The lake was beautiful. [ ]
3 Yar lived on an island. [ ]
4 A fireball destroyed the island. [ ]
5 Baylene crashed into the sky. [ ]
6 There was a fireball in the sky. [ ]

9 Match the words.

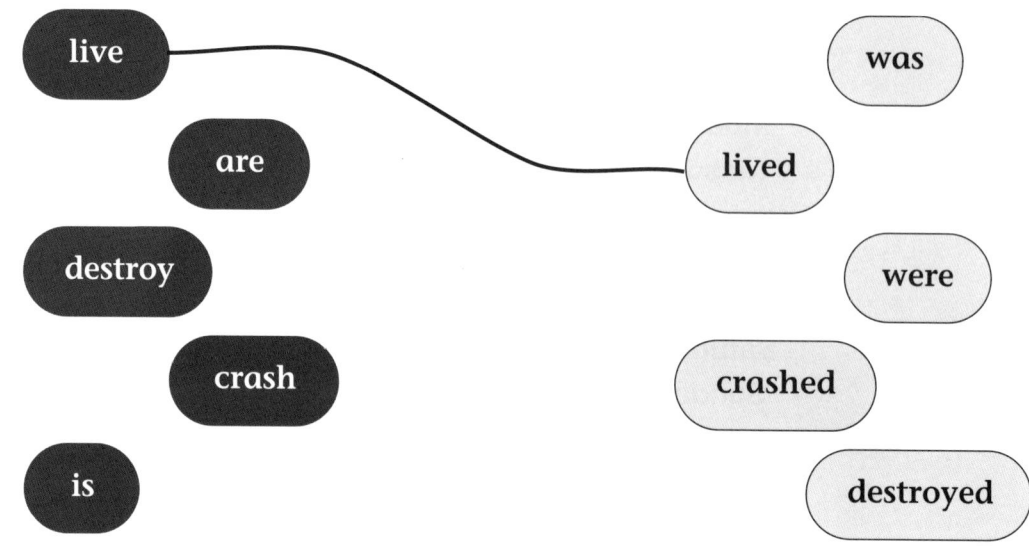

10 **Write the verbs in the past tense.**

There (be) ____were____ (1) black clouds in the sky. It (be) _____ (2) windy too. A giant thunderbolt (crash) _____ (3) in the sky. The storm (destroy) _____ (4) the city. It (be) _____ (5) not a good year for the people.

11 **Listen. Tick the words you hear.**

- ☐ volcano
- ☐ scared
- ☐ rocks
- ☐ alive
- ☐ hot
- ☐ noise
- ☐ ash
- ☐ lucky
- ☐ storm

12 **Write words from Activity 11 in the sentences.**

1 The ____volcano____ erupted.
2 Grey _____ covered the houses.
3 The animals were _____ .
4 Cleo the cat was _____ .
5 Her home was under the _____ .
6 She was _____ .

13 Label the pictures.

sky
ash
pelican
~~volcano~~
sea

1 _Volcano_ 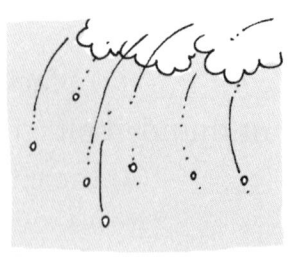   2  _____   3 _____

4 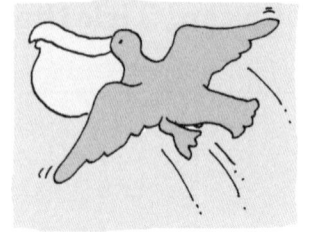 _____   5 _____

14 Find and write the sentences.

1 the   ocean   sailed   sailors   The
The sailors sailed the ocean.

2 on   They   the   arrived   island
_____ .

3 There   on   rats   were   the   boat
_____ .

4 food   The   wanted   rats
_____ .

5 eggs   destroyed   They   tortoises'   the
_____ .

15 Choose and complete.

hungry   horrid   black   lonely

1 George was _____ .
2 The volcano was _____ .
3 The goats were _____ .
4 The rats were _____ .

16 **Complete the words.**

a　o　e
　　　　o
i　　i
　o　u

```
        w
          f
  n   l h       s
  d r     g h t
        r
        d r     r
                m
        c
        n
```

17 **Write the years in numbers and words.**

1 Two thousand and twenty _____

2 Nineteen ninety-seven _____

3 2004 _____

4 1993 _____

18 **Circle the verbs in the past tense.**

| lived | crash | destroyed | arrive | wanted |
| happened | emptied | sail | covered |

19 **Complete with *was* or *were*.**

There _____ (1) a giant tortoise. He _____ (2) sad! There _____ (3) pelicans and there _____ (4) hungry goats. I _____ (5) scared of them, but I _____ (6) more scared of the rats.

English Adventure

Self evaluation. Read, think and shade the YES.

I can

describe events in the past. Y E S

say the date (year). Y E S

talk about unusual weather. Y E S

Make a word and complete the sentence.

I'm good at _ _ _ _ _ _ _ _ _ .

H E G I L
N S

6 Flying high

1 Can you remember? Write *true* (T) or *false* (F)?

1 Ben's kite crashed. [T]
2 Tessa wanted to phone her mum. [ ]
3 The Wright Brothers invented mobile phones. [ ]
4 The name *Icarus* was on the kite. [ ]
5 Oscar arrived with his tennis racket. [ ]

2 Look at the picture and correct the sentences.

1 It rained yesterday! — *It didn't rain yesterday!*
2 The children went to the sports centre. — _____.
3 They arrived at three o'clock. — _____.
4 They were happy! — _____!

3 Listen and answer.

1 Where did uncle Harry go?
_____.

2 What was the weather like?
_____.

3 What time did he arrive?
_____.

4 What's wrong?

1850

1. <u>They didn't have mobile phones in 1850!</u>
2. _____ !
3. _____ !
4. _____ !
5. _____ !

5 Use a mirror and write the message.

The Wright brothers changed the world.

_____ .

Do you agree?

☐ Yes, they did.   ☐ No, they didn't.

6 Who's speaking? B.E.N., Jim, or John?

1 He made a trap!

2 Let's get out of here!

3 We're rich!

4 What did he do?

5 I can't remember ...

7 Can you remember? Answer the questions.

1 Where did Jim and John Silver go? _____.
2 Who was in the room? _____.
3 Was he dead or alive? _____.
4 What was in Captain Flint's hand? _____.
5 What two things did B.E.N. remember? _____.

8 What's inside your treasure chest? Draw and write.

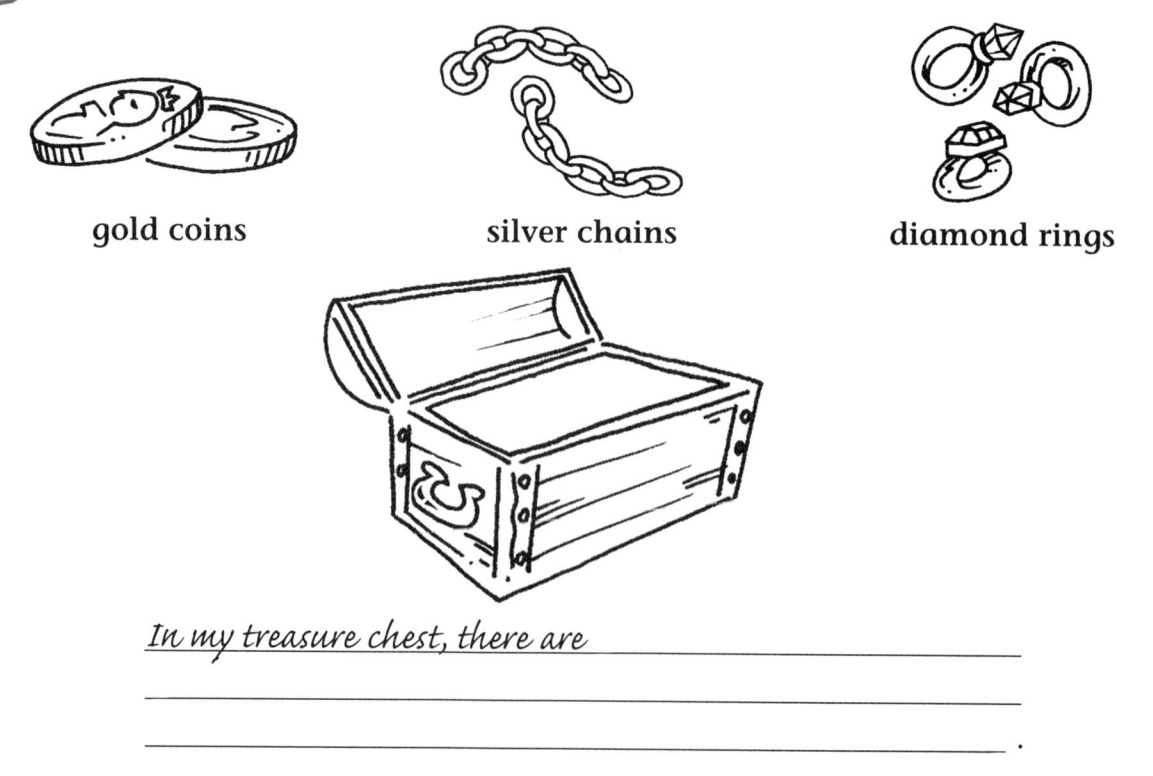

gold coins   silver chains   diamond rings

In my treasure chest, there are _____
_____
_____.

9 Write the questions and match to the correct answers.

1. Did fly Icarus want to ?
   <u>Did Icarus want to fly?</u> ?

2. Did he a kite make ?
   _____ ?

3. work a in ? Did he shop bicycle
   _____ ?

4. fly Did too he sun ? near the
   _____ ?

5. wings ? make he Did
   _____ ?

6. Brazil fly ? he Did to
   _____ ?

Yes, he did.

No, he didn't.

10 What did they make? Look and write.

1. <u>I made a canoe</u>.

2. _____.

3. _____.

4. _____.

11 How did they make it? Look and write.

wood

paper

modelling clay

1. <u>Oscar made the canoe from modelling clay.</u>
2. _____.
3. _____.
4. _____.

43

12 Can you remember? Read and tick the correct people.

He / They	Grandad	Wright brothers	Both
invented new things.			
worked in a bicycle shop.			
flew a kite.			
had fun!			

13 What did Oscar and his family do? Listen and circle.

On **Saturday** / **(Sunday)**, we went by **train** / **bike** to the **river** / **beach**. In the **afternoon** / **evening**, we visited **cousin Larry** / **auntie Fay**. We didn't go to **Grandad's** / **the shops**. There wasn't **a bus** / **time**. We arrived home at **nine** / **ten** o'clock. We watched a **video** / **DVD** and went to bed.

14 Write the story from Activity 13. Choose the same words or change them.

_____
_____
_____
_____

15 Find and write ten verbs.

S	A	I	L	H	S	E	C
L	R	X	M	A	K	E	H
W	R	D	C	V	B	N	A
A	I	N	V	E	N	T	N
T	V	S	Q	F	L	Y	G
C	E	G	O	Y	S	E	E
H	L	W	O	R	K	Y	W

sail
_____
_____
_____
_____
_____
_____
_____
_____
_____

Now write the verbs in the past.

16 Complete the sentences.

1 I didn't go to the beach.   _I went to the mountains._
2 I didn't make a plane.   _____.
3 I didn't invent a bicycle.   _____.
4 I didn't work in a school.   _____.
5 I didn't arrive at 5 o'clock.   _____.

17 Write the questions and answers.

1 Did you play football yesterday? — Yes, I did.

2 _____ — _____

3 _____ — _____

English Adventure

Self evaluation. Read, think and shade the YES.

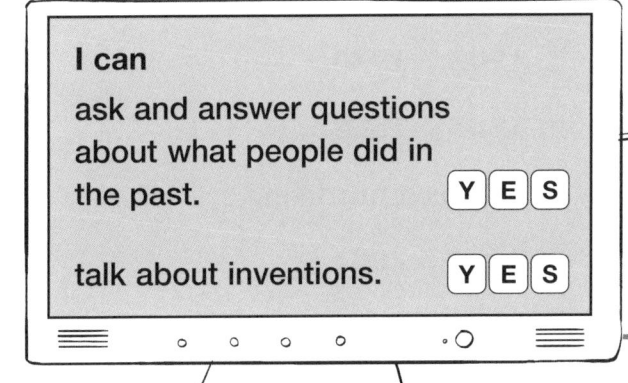

I can
ask and answer questions about what people did in the past.   Y E S

talk about inventions.   Y E S

Make two words and complete the sentence.

English _ _ _ _ _ _.

F I U S N

Review
Units 5 and 6

1 Read and draw the weather symbols on the map.

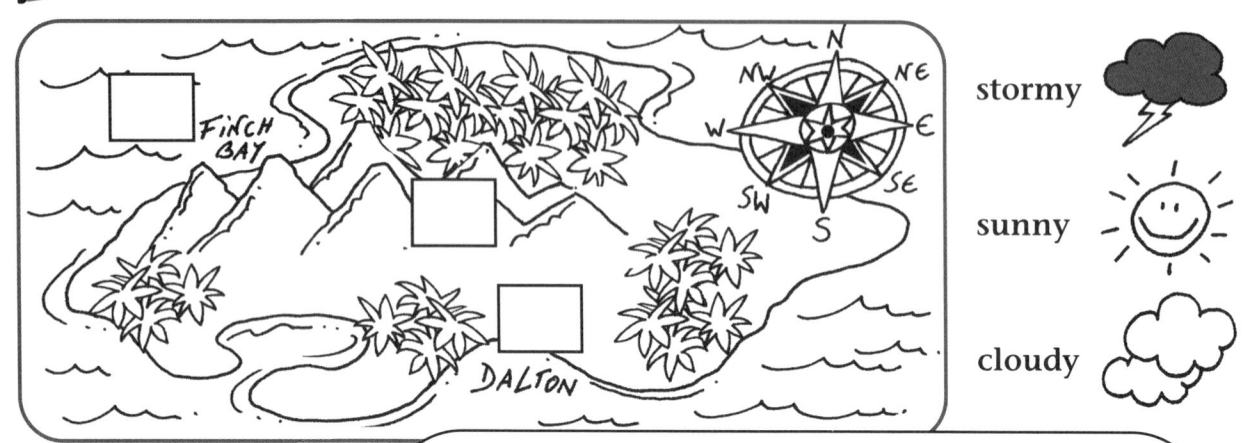

stormy

sunny

cloudy

Yesterday, there was a storm at Finch Bay. It didn't rain in the mountains but it was cold and cloudy. In Dalton it was cold too, but it was very sunny.

2 Look at the weather map and complete.

1 There was a _____ at _____ .
2 It didn't rain in _____ .
3 It was _____ in the _____ .
4 In Dalton it _____ .
5 It _____ stormy in Dalton.

3 Listen, match and circle the correct dates.

1 In **1987 / 1990**
2 There were storms
3 The brothers flew
4 In **1963 / 1861**
5 They invented tyres

a in **1903 / 1930**.
b in **1808 / 1888**.
c there was a hurricane.
d in **2002 / 2001**.
e the winter was cold.

46

4. What does Granny remember? Look and complete.

My school _was_ (1) lovely! There _____ (2) two big windows. Under the window there _____ (3) a place for bicycles. There _____ (4) cows in the field, and there _____ (5) a tree in the garden. There _____ (6) a dog too. His name _____ (7) Timmy.

5. Read and match.

1. Was your school big?
2. Where did you play?
3. Was the dog friendly?
4. Did you have a bike?
5. Did you like school?

a. Yes, but he was very old.
b. Yes, I did.
c. No, it wasn't. There were two classrooms.
d. In the garden. There wasn't a playground.
e. Yes, I did.

6. Choose and write your story.

One day a **reporter / pop star** went to a **café / restaurant** with a **friend / neighbour**. It was **cold / sunny**. They went by **train / car**. They wanted a **cake / drink**. Under the table there was a **box / bag**. They opened it! Inside there was a **snake / treasure map**!

One day _____

_____

_____

_____ .

7 Stars in their eyes

1 Look and write the answers.

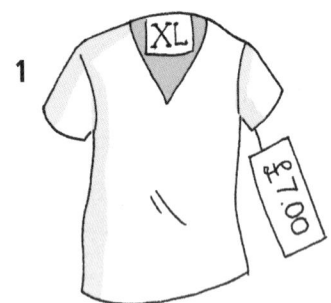

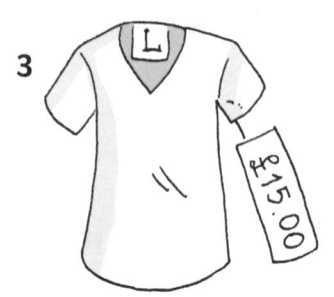

1. Which is the biggest T-shirt? _Number 1_
2. Which is the most expensive? _____
3. Which is the smallest? _____
4. Which is the cheapest? _____

2 Complete the chart.

	expensive	more expensive	the most expensive
	cheap		

good, bigger, cheaper, the biggest

better, the cheapest, big, best

3 Add prices and complete the sentences.

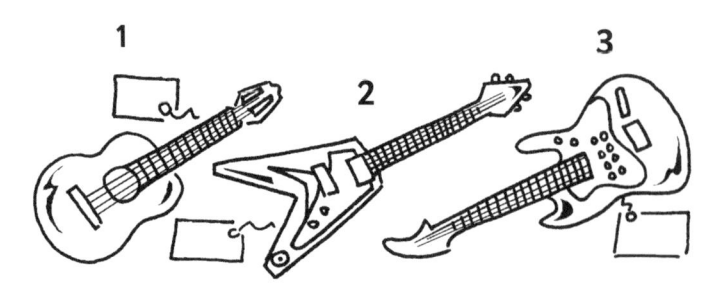

Guitar ____ is the _____.
Guitar ____ is the _____.
The best is Guitar ____.
Is the best the most expensive?
_____.

48

4. Find the opposites.

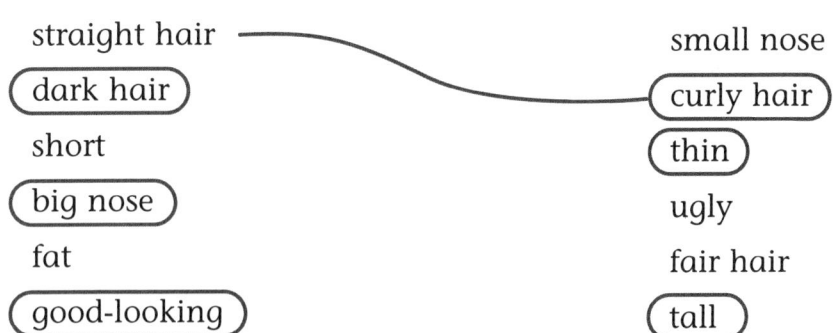

straight hair — curly hair
dark hair
short
big nose
fat
good-looking

small nose
thin
ugly
fair hair
tall

5. What does Ivan look like? Read and draw.

Read the words in circles in Activity 4. These words describe Ivan, the missing pop star from *Top Trio*. Draw his picture in the middle.

6. Write about *Top Trio*.

fattest   best-looking   shortest   ~~tallest~~   thinnest

1 *Fin is the tallest.*
2 _____ .
3 _____ .
4 _____ .
5 _____ .

7 Write the sentences correctly.

1 Stitch   guitar   played   the
   Stitch played the guitar.

2 loud   It   very   was
   _____.

3 good   It   wasn't
   _____.

4 louder   the   He   guitar   played
   _____.

5 but   louder   better   it   It   was   wasn't
   _____.

6 was   It   !   worse
   _____!

7 music   world   worst   !   in   It   the   was   the
   _____!

8 Match the opposites.

good
better
the best

the worst
bad
worse

9 Complete.

I can make the _____ coffee on Hawaii!

That's the _____ music in the world!

Who's speaking? Write the name. _____

50

10 Find and write the words.

1 riutag
2 dmru
3 uetlf
4 iivlno
5 npoai

11 Music Quiz. Ask a friend and complete the quiz.

		me	my friend
1 When do you listen to music?	a in the car	☐	☐
	b when you study	☐	☐
	c when you relax	☐	☐
2 How do you learn best?	a with music	☐	☐
	b in silence	☐	☐
	c with the TV	☐	☐
	d with the radio	☐	☐
3 What music do you like best?	a pop	☐	☐
	b rock	☐	☐
	c classical	☐	☐
	d other	☐	☐

12 Which group do you like best? Draw and write.

Make a poster for your favourite group's next concert.
Then answer the questions.

1 How much are the cheapest tickets?
   _____.

2 How much are the most expensive tickets?
   _____.

13 **Match and write.**

1 She sailed
2 He flew
3 She explored
4 He climbed

a the fastest plane.
b the greatest ocean.
c the highest mountain.
d the longest river.

1 _____.
2 _____.
3 _____.
4 _____.

14 **Read and write.**

In your country, which is

the biggest city? _____
the highest mountain? _____
the longest river? _____
the most beautiful place to visit? _____
the most famous monument? _____

15 **Listen and write the prices.**

1 Which seat is the cheapest? _____
2 Which seat is the most expensive? _____

PRICE: _____
_____
_____

52

16. Find the words and label the pictures.

```
C H E A P E S T R I
P L M O U N T A I N
H L S U M E L L V O
I T A C S P W O E G
G K X N T I T N R U
H Z F W E H C G F I
E R Y F A S T E S T
S D N A M T D S B A
T L O U D E S T W R
```

highest — mountain

_____ — _____

_____ — _____

_____ — _____

_____ — _____

17. Complete the chart.

| better | good | | | worse |
| the best | | | the worst | bad |

18. Look and complete.

_____'s got the longest name.
Tina's got the _____ shoes.
Tracy's _____ the _____ hair. The tallest girl is _____.

English Adventure

Self evaluation. Read, think and shade the YES.

I can

describe people. Y E S

compare more than two things. Y E S

Make a word and complete the sentence.

I like English _ _ _ _ _ _ _ _ _ _ _ .

D N A U R
V E T E

8 Journeys

1 Read and answer.

> Oh, no!   Oh, good!

1 We're going to miss the bus! _____
2 We're going to swim in the sea. _____
3 We're going to eat paella. _____
4 We're going to have a holiday. _____
5 We're going to climb a mountain. _____
6 We're going to visit a monument. _____

2 Read and match. Write another sentence for each place.

- I've got Maths today!
- I want to take a photo.
- _____

on holiday
in school

- Let's have an ice cream.
- We've got Art this afternoon.
- _____

3 Complete the questionnaire and ask a friend.

On holiday, are you going to   you a friend

1 swim in the sea? ☐ ☐
2 buy souvenirs? ☐ ☐
3 visit monuments? ☐ ☐
4 go on a plane? ☐ ☐
5 _____ ☐ ☐

54

4 Classify.

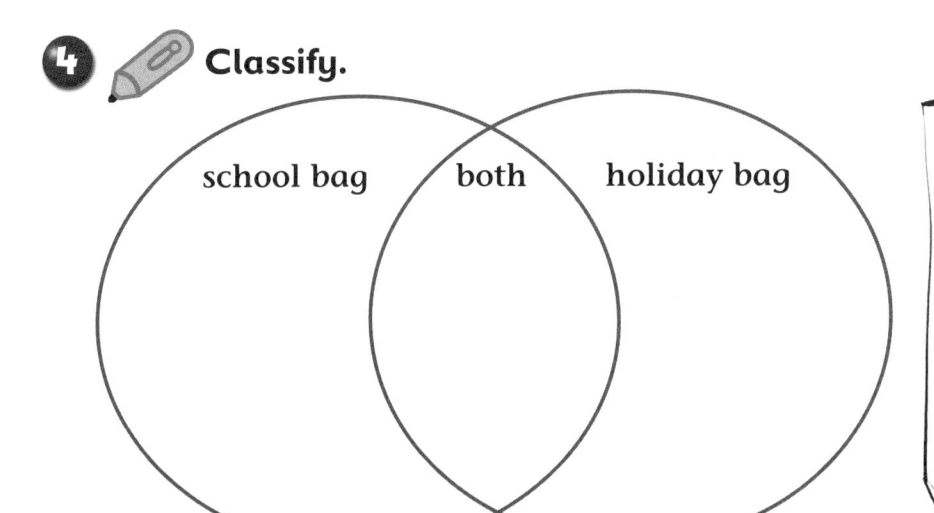

school bag | both | holiday bag

torch   sunglasses
sweets   pen
flippers   sharpener
ruler   pencil case
camera   rubber
book

5 Match and write.

1 Where did they go?   a By plane.
2 When did they go?   b To Spain.
3 How did they go?   c On Monday.
4 What did they do?   d They had fun.

1 <u>The children went on holiday</u> .
2 _____ .
3 _____ .
4 _____ .

6 Where's the hotel? Read and mark the route.

Cross the bridge, walk up the road, turn left, then right. The hotel is on a small street on the left.

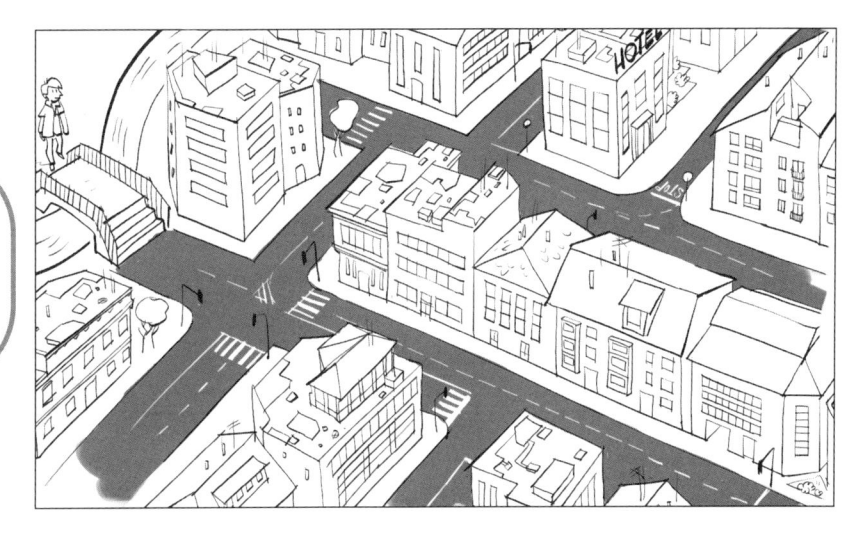

7 **Write the questions correctly. Then find the answers in the story.**

you pack Did your Milo? bags

1 _____ ?
  _____ .

did you Why Atlantis? to here come

2 _____ ?
  _____ .

are you What going to money? with your do all

3 _____ ?
  _____ .

8 **Write *true* (T) or *false* (F)?**

1 Milo didn't pack his bag. ☐ T
2 Milo's going to open a restaurant. ☐
3 Milo doesn't need his old job. ☐
4 He's going to stay with Kida. ☐
5 Milo wanted to get rich. ☐
6 He's going to stay in Atlantis. ☐
7 He's going to be happy. ☐

9 **Order and write the true sentences from Activity 8.**

_____ .
_____ .
_____ .
_____ .

10 Making butter. Read and complete.

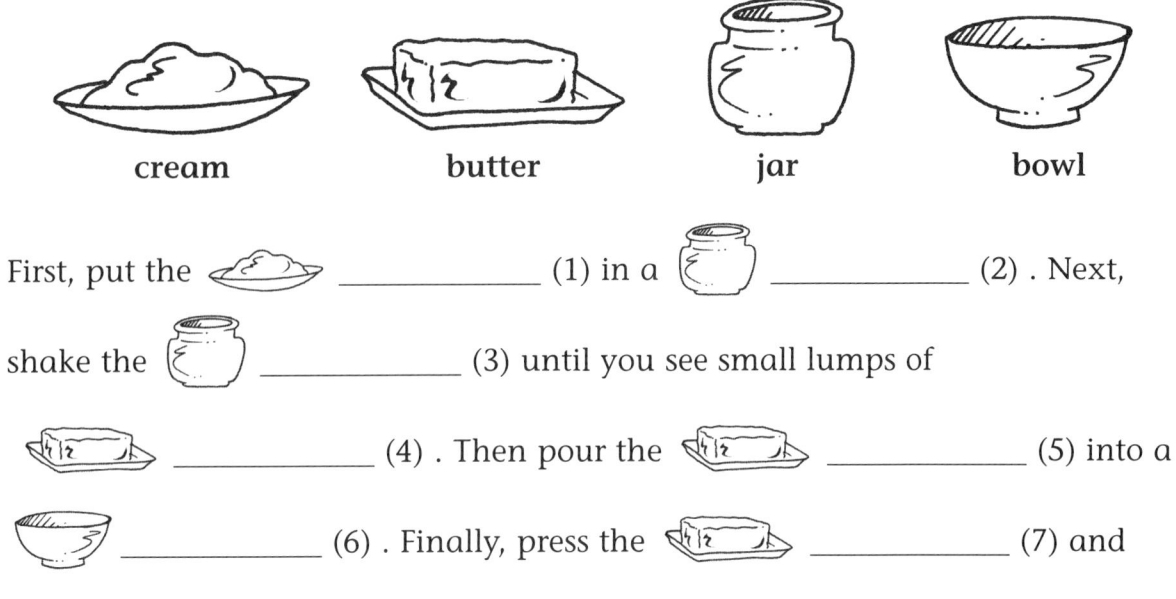

cream   butter   jar   bowl

First, put the _____ (1) in a _____ (2) . Next, shake the _____ (3) until you see small lumps of _____ (4) . Then pour the _____ (5) into a _____ (6) . Finally, press the _____ (7) and separate the liquid.

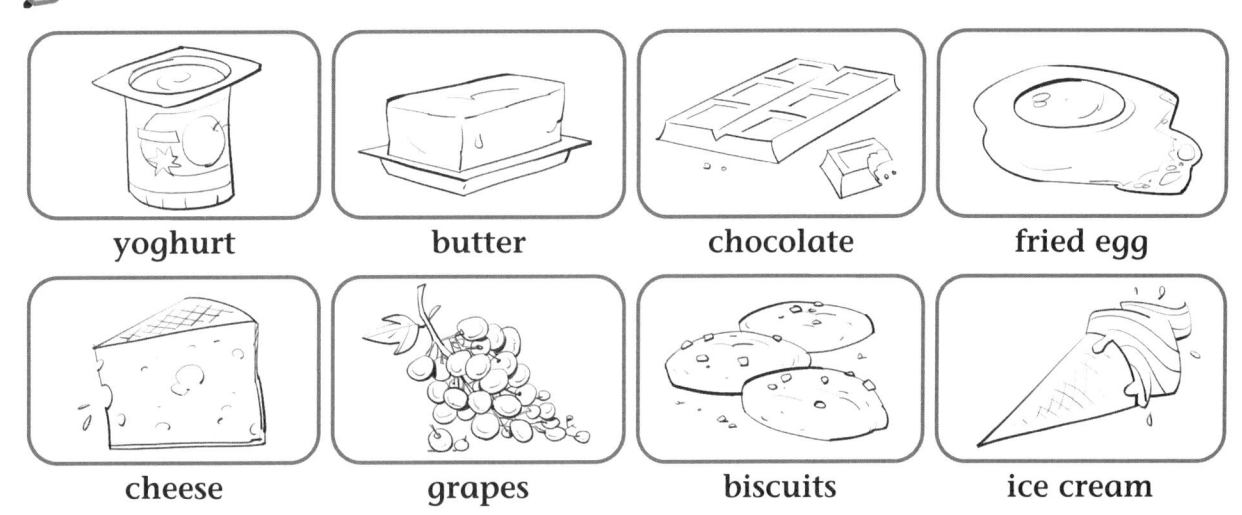

11 Circle the foods that contain milk.

yoghurt   butter   chocolate   fried egg

cheese   grapes   biscuits   ice cream

12 Listen, draw and label.

13 Write the words in the pyramid.

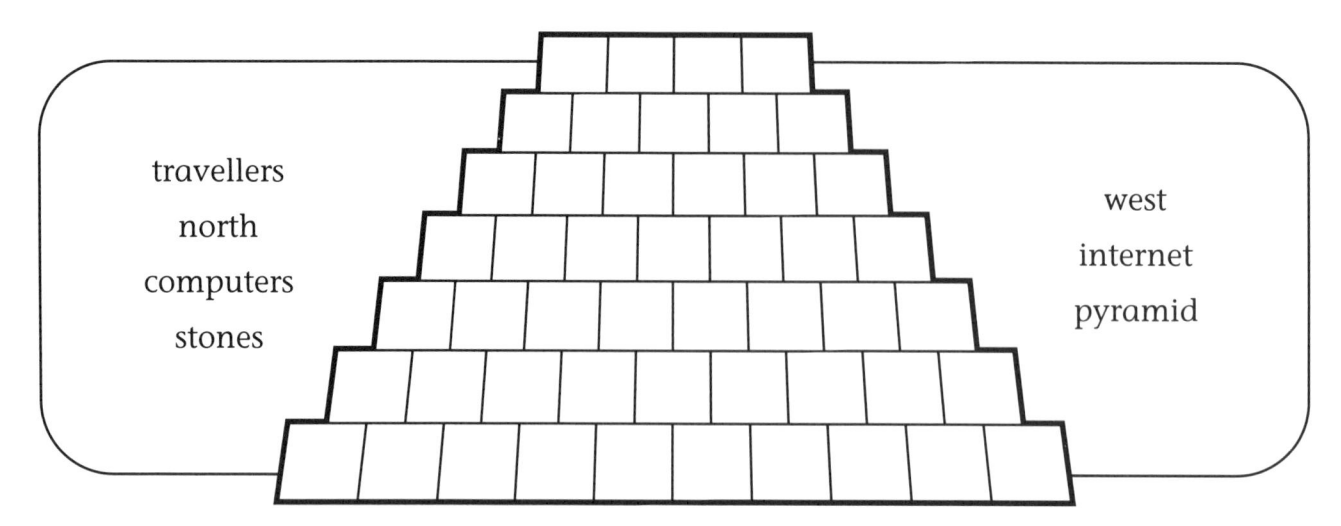

travellers
north
computers
stones

west
internet
pyramid

14 Write the words from the pyramid in the text.

_____ (1) come from all over the world to see the Great _____ (2) in Egypt. They come from the _____ (3), the south, the east and the _____ (4). The Egyptians carried the heavy _____ (5) with no machines. They didn't have _____ (6) to help them make drawings of the pyramids. Find out more on the _____ (7) !

15 Complete.

Across
1 Italians are from …
4 The pyramids are in …
5 Giant pandas are from …

Down
2 Marco Polo travelled to …
3 They eat paella in …

58

16 Read and match.

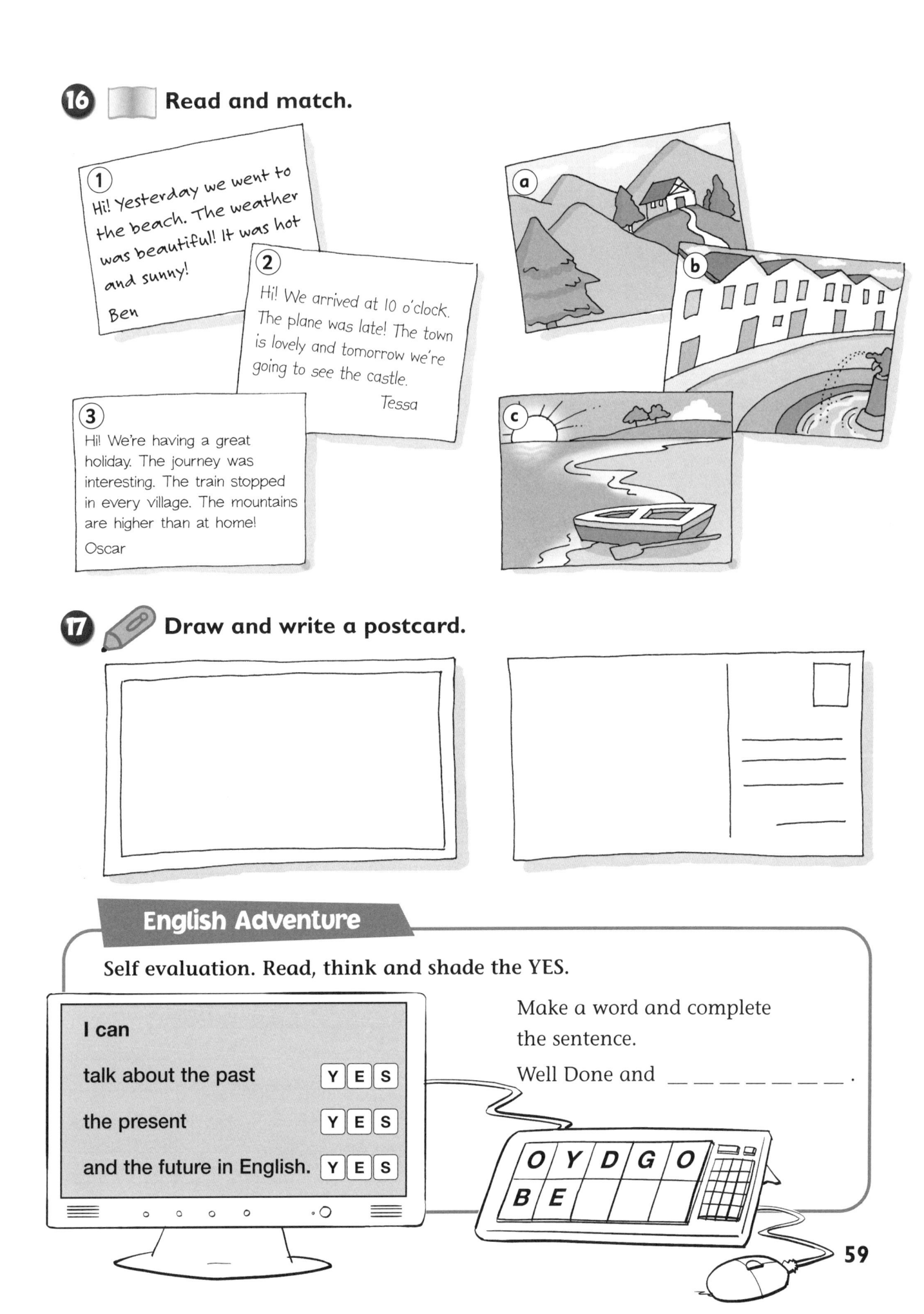

1. Hi! Yesterday we went to the beach. The weather was beautiful! It was hot and sunny!
Ben

2. Hi! We arrived at 10 o'clock. The plane was late! The town is lovely and tomorrow we're going to see the castle.
Tessa

3. Hi! We're having a great holiday. The journey was interesting. The train stopped in every village. The mountains are higher than at home!
Oscar

17 Draw and write a postcard.

English Adventure

Self evaluation. Read, think and shade the YES.

I can

talk about the past Y E S

the present Y E S

and the future in English. Y E S

Make a word and complete the sentence.

Well Done and _____.

O Y D G O
B E

Review
Units 7 and 8

1 Write.

| weakest | shortest | ~~tallest~~ | strongest | fattest | thinnest |

1 Bongo is the _tallest._
2 Sparky is the _____.
3 Bongo is the _____.
4 Sparky is the _____.
5 Sparky is the _____.
6 Bongo is the _____.

Bongo   Sparky

2 Write.

What is Oscar going to take on holiday?

He is going to take _____
_____
_____
_____
_____
_____
_____
_____
_____
_____ .

3. Write.

1 (stellat) _tallest_

13 (rohssett) _____

Christmas

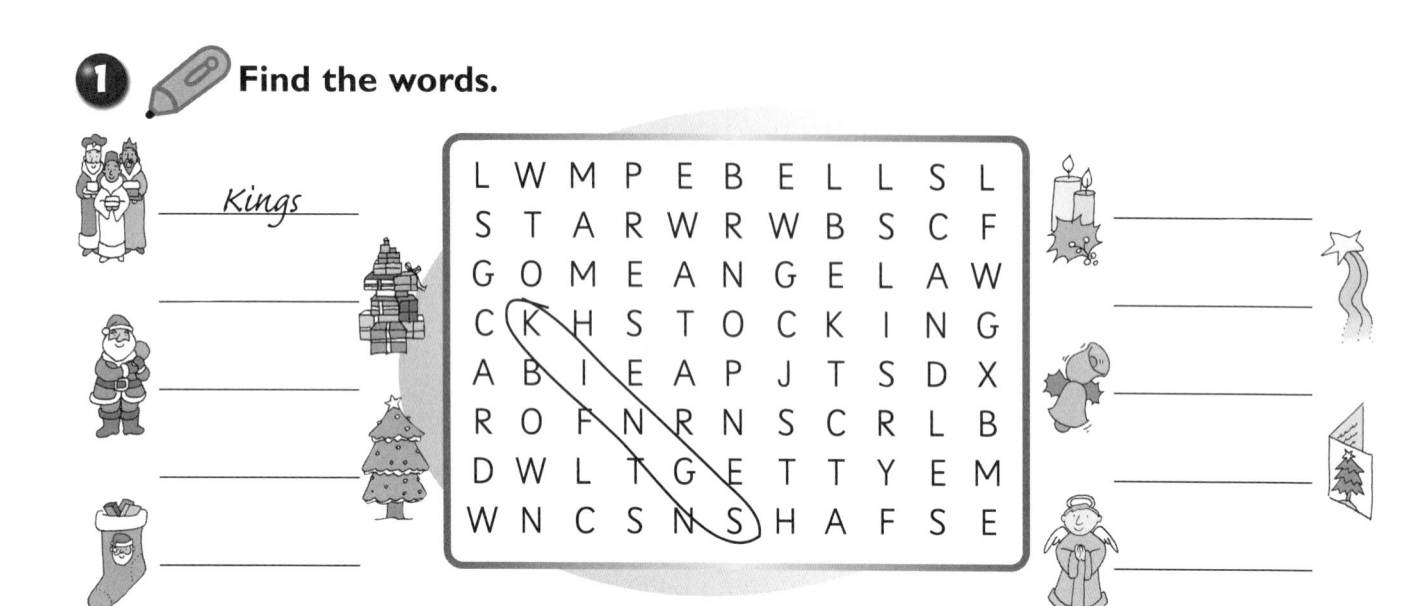

1 Find the words.

Kings

```
L W M P E B E L L S L
S T A R W R W B S C F
G O M E A N G E L A W
C K H S T O C K I N G
A B I E A P J T S D X
R O F N R N S C R L B
D W L T G E T T Y E M
W N C S N S H A F S E
```

2 Who gets which present? Find and write.

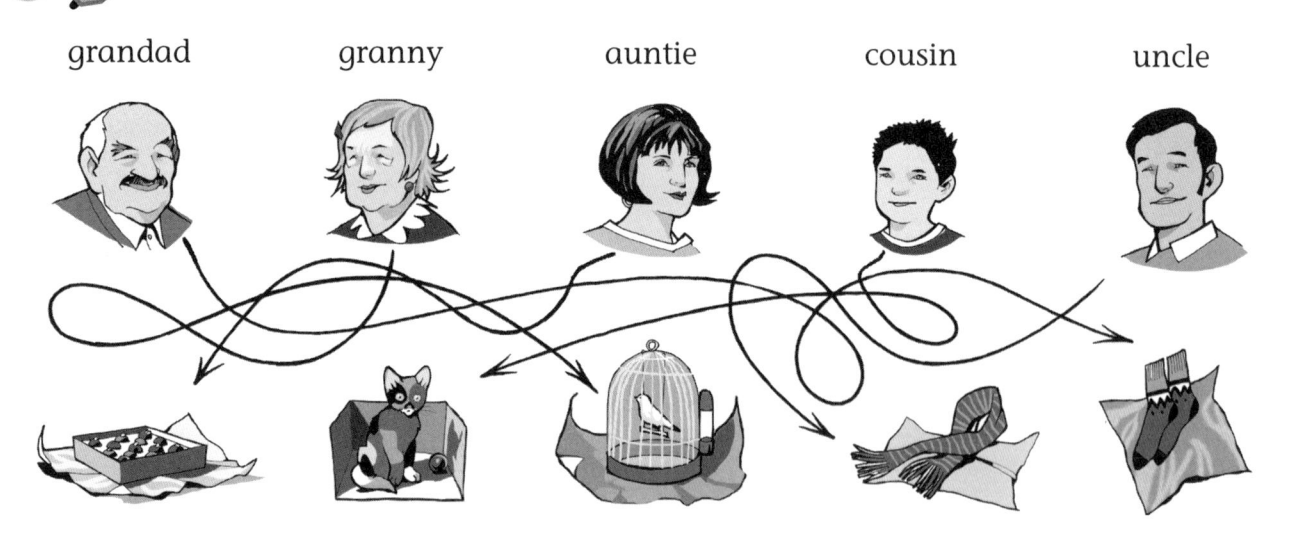

grandad   granny   auntie   cousin   uncle

1 _Grandad gets socks._
2 _____.
3 _____.
4 _____.
5 _____.

62

Valentine's Day

1 Valentine's messages. Match and write.

1 You're a
2 I like your
3 You've got
4 You're very

a eyes.
b kind and helpful.
c good friend.
d a lovely smile.

1 _____ .
2 _____ .
3 _____ .
4 _____ .

2 Listen and order.

☐ I like your smile
☐ Roses are red
☐ And I like you
☐ Violets are blue

3 Find the words and complete.

We celebrate Valentine's Day in y e r u b r F a _____ .

St Valentine was from y t I l a _____ .

Today we send l f o w s r e _____ .

and h a c l o c o t s e _____ .

to the people we v o e l _____ .

63

Earth Day

1 Circle the people who celebrate Earth Day.

2 Are you Earth-friendly? Ask and answer with a friend.

	you	a friend
1 Do you recycle paper?		
2 Do you save water?		
3 Do you pick up your rubbish?		
4 Do you recycle glass bottles?		
5 Do you respect trees and plants?		

3 What more can you do to help the planet?

I can _____

_____

_____ .